Butterflies From Heaven

A Children's Book That Heals Hearts

By Jennifer Minnite

Illustrated by Manuela Soriani

Dedicated to our butterflies from heaven,
Lucca Matteo Minnite and Stan Bledsoe — a.k.a. "Pop".

J.M.

To my mom, Silvana. You made me strong.

M.S.

Sophia's eyes fluttered open. Today was her first day back at school.

"I'm not ready," she whispered to herself, "but I'm going to try."

Sophia yawned, slid out from her blankets, and softly walked to her bedroom window. She opened it wide, took a deep breath, and let the sun wash over her face.

Flash! A bright blue butterfly flew into her room! It landed on the picture frame showing Sophia holding her baby brother, Lucca. Sophia tiptoed towards the butterfly. Her heart fluttered and goose bumps ran up and down her legs. It made her feel good, even on the inside.

"Sophia, breakfast," her mom called from downstairs.

"Just a minute." Sophia didn't want to leave this butterfly for anything.

"*Sunday* breakfast," added her dad.

A delicious smell of bacon, syrup, and buttery pancakes drifted upstairs.

"Coming!" said Sophia.

She pulled on her favorite outfit and matching boots. She left her window open for the butterfly, still perched over her picture of her baby brother.

"Bye, bye, butterfly!" Sophia sang down the stairs, hoping very much she would see it again.

The family kitchen was cozy. Bright yellow curtains caught the sunlight and checkered place mats circled the wooden table in front of each chair.

Sunday breakfast on a Monday morning was a very special thing. Sophia's dad wore the paper tie she had made him for Father's Day. Over the tie, he wore Mom's pink apron.

"I didn't want to get blueberry syrup on my special tie," he laughed and gave her a kiss. Sophia wrapped her arms around him. His big smile made wrinkles around his eyes.

"Eat your pancakes, kiddo," her dad said and served her a short stack.

Sophia plopped into her mom's lap.

"Good morning. How did you sleep?" Mom asked.

"It was quiet again last night," Sophia said simply.

"I know, sweetie. It was quiet for all of us," Mom said and rubbed Sophia's back.

Sophia reached for two chocolate chips, a strawberry, and blueberry syrup to make a happy face. Maybe that would help. She knew she wasn't ready to go back to school. But she would keep her promise; she was going to try.

"I'm done!" said her older brother Giovanni, pushing his plate back. "I have something for you, Sophia." He slid a bright blue rock across the table. Sophia gasped.

"That's your lucky rock! For me?" she said.

"It's for good luck," he said with a sweet shrug.

"Thank you!" she said.

The blue rock reminded Sophia of the butterfly. Immediately, she got another fluttery feeling and more goose bumps.

"This morning the most beautiful butterfly flew right into my room and landed on the picture frame of me holding Baby Lucca!" she told everyone.

Dad squeezed Mom's shoulders. "That's one special butterfly!" he cheered.

Dad checked his watch. "Time to go. Looks like Sunday breakfast was good to the last drop!"

At the bottom of the hill on the way to school, Sophia spotted the blue butterfly.

"Mom, there it is! Just waiting!"

"Are you sure it's the same butterfly?"

"I know it is because I have that fluttery feeling in my heart and more goose bumps!"

Her mom looked at her own arms. "I've got goose bumps, too... the ones that let you know something very special just happened."

Sophia liked the idea that this butterfly was following her. She hoped it would stay the whole day.

Sophia's teacher greeted her on the playground.

"Welcome back," she said and gave Sophia a hug.

"Thank you," smiled Sophia.

Her mom said goodbye with a butterfly kiss on Sophia's cheek.

Then she whispered, "You know, even I'm feeling more fluttery."

After recess, everyone gathered on the reading rug. This was Sophia's favorite time of day at school. She loved listening to her teacher read.

Today Sophia got to choose the story - the one about the caterpillar turning into a butterfly. The ending was always perfect... "Just then the caterpillar closed his eyes and he became a beautiful butterfly." Sophia's heart fluttered.

She looked up and there it was! The bright blue butterfly was just outside the nearest window. This definitely was one special butterfly!

After school, Nana was waiting. Sophia spotted Nana's convertible bug ready to pick her up. "Hop in!" Nana greeted.

Nana wore her bright blue muumuu and big bug-eyed sunglasses. Her arms opened wide in a big hug and Sophia felt like she was in the wings of a butterfly. Then Nana handed Sophia matching sunglasses and they zoomed down the street.

"How did school go today?" Nana yelled over the roar of the engine.

"Okay," Sophia said softly.

Nana's brow wrinkled with some heavy thinking. Then she took a surprise sudden left turn!

"Where are we going?" Sophia asked.

"Some place very special. I think you'll like it."

Just as they were turning, Sophia glanced up. There it was ... her bright blue butterfly and the fluttery feeling too!

"There's my butterfly!" Sophia exclaimed.

"I have a hunch that your butterfly is a butterfly from heaven," Nana said with a wink. "Every time you see it, it's giving you a big angel kiss."

"It's been following me around all day!"

"That's what butterflies from heaven do," said Nana.

Sophia and Nana arrived at a beautiful meadow. Holding hands, they walked over to a bench waiting just for them. Colorful wildflowers had bloomed and birds chirped sweet songs. Nana gently grasped Sophia's hands and she took a deep breath.

"Sophia, there's more to tell about butterflies from heaven. When someone dies, even though we can't see them here, they can come back to visit people they love. After "Pop" died, I was very sad. Often I came to this meadow and this very bench to think about him. The first time I sat on this bench, a magnificent yellow butterfly landed on my shoulder. It stayed until I realized it was a butterfly from heaven... It was "Pop" giving me an angel kiss and reminding me that he is always here in spirit."

Three tears ran down her soft face.

"Nana, is my butterfly really a butterfly from heaven?"

"Yes, Sophia."

"Is my butterfly Baby Lucca?"

"You betcha!" Nana nodded.

"How do I know it's not just another butterfly?"

"Butterflies from heaven give angel kisses that feel fluttery, just like goose bumps," explained Nana.

"Just butterflies?" Sophia wondered.

"For you and me, it's butterflies, because we love them so much. For others, it can be a beautiful sunset, or a certain snowflake that lands on your nose, or a flower that bends in your direction. Our loved ones will always find ways to visit us to give us angel kisses," Nana said, and she hugged Sophia.

"There it is again," whispered Sophia pointing to her butterfly.
As it floated above, a bigger yellow butterfly circled around it.
"I've got goose bumps," said Nana and Sophia giggled.
"Definitely our lucky day," said Nana. "Time to go home."
"Bye, bye butterfly," said Sophia. "See you soon."

Sophia opened the front door. Instantly, the smell of Mom's spaghetti sauce tickled her tummy. Giovanni's rock music blared from his music player. Sophia relaxed. The house was alive again.

"We're back," Nana called out, "and we're hungry!"

"I think Sophia should share what she learned today," said Nana at dinner. Sophia's face lit up. She told everyone again about the bright blue butterfly that had followed her all day.

"It was really a butterfly from heaven. It was Lucca's spirit coming to give me angel kisses."

Her Dad agreed. "Today on my bike ride there was an extra special wind at my back, blowing me faster than I had ever ridden before. I knew Baby Lucca's spirit was with me."

"I got a fluttery feeling when I gave you my lucky rock this morning," Giovanni said.

"Tonight I know that Lucca is visiting us," added Mom softly.

After dinner, Nana said her goodbyes. It was time for bed. They all gathered on Sophia's bed for a bedtime story.

"I think Sophia should tell the story tonight," said Giovanni. "It's been her lucky day."

Sophia had the perfect story to tell. "Once there was a baby boy who was with us for a few days. Then he got sick so he had to go back up to heaven. But he visits his family whenever he misses us and visits whenever we miss him. He loves watching us from heaven. He always shows up in special ways to give us angel kisses."

Sophia pulled the covers up to her chin. Before she fell asleep, she reached over to her nightstand and picked up Lucca's picture frame. She brought it to her face and gave his tiny cheek a gentle butterfly kiss.

"Good night butterfly," she said holding the frame to her chest.

She drifted off to sleep, dreaming of her butterfly from heaven.

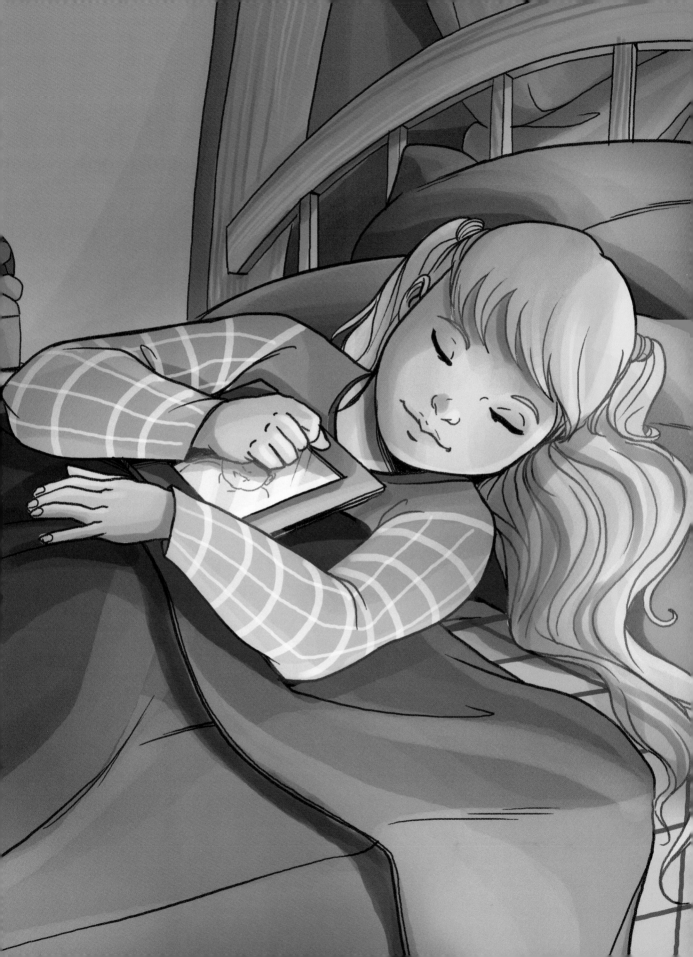

Butterflies From Heaven

Text by Jennifer Minnite

Illustrations by Manuela Soriani

©2012 Jennifer Minnite

www.mybutterfliesfromheaven.com

Library of congress cataloging-in-publication data is available

ISBN 978-0-9849168-0-1

First edition, 2012

Lightning Source Inc. 1246 Heil Quaker Blvd.

La Vergne, TN 37086 United States

Jennifer Minnite

JENNIFER MINNITE was an elementary school teacher for eight years before becoming a mom.

Her Butterflies From Heaven series was inspired by her son Lucca. Born with a rare heart defect, Lucca lived for twelve short days, but his spirit is often felt in wonderful ways. Jennifer lives in Pleasanton, California with her husband, their three children, and their one special butterfly from heaven.

Manuela Soriani

MANUELA SORIANI has been a student and an office employee. She has experience as a comic book artist and is a successful children's book illustrator.

Manuela wants to thank Jennifer for trusting her skills and sensibility for such an important project. This book has a personal meaning for Manuela also. Her mother passed away after a long illness when she was just 15, and is still deeply missed. Manuela lives with her husband and two cats in the small town of Castelmassa in Northern Italy, where she was born and raised.